Sound Engii

MW01069666

By
James E. Britton

Table Of Contents:

Introduction

Chapter One: How Do We Define Sound?

Chapter Two: Graphs, Frequency, and Amplitude

Chapter Three: The Speed of Sound and Wavelength

Chapter Four: Phase

Chapter Five: Harmonics

Chapter Six: Envelope

Chapter Seven: AMPLITUDE: The Loudness of Sound

Chapter Eight: Electrical Sound Waves

Chapter Nine: Controlling Sound in the Recording Environment

Chapter Ten: The Loudness of Sound

Chapter Eleven: How we Hear Sound

Chapter Twelve: Frequency Response

Chapter 13: Flat Frequency Response

Chapter Fourteen: The Frequency Spectrum

Chapter Fifteen: The Recording Chain

Introduction

Hello, and welcome to this book that will cover the basics of sound for recording and sound engineering. Together, we'll learn about the principles of sound as they relate to recording. I'll be telling you more about my background shortly, but first let's take a look at what this book is all about.

This book is for anyone who wishes to build a foundation of the theory of sound in order to make better sound recordings. This book DOES NOT cover principles of recording itself, but will give you the fundamentals of what sound actually is in order to be able to be prepared to engineer and manipulate the sounds you will be recording.

First thing's first: CONGRATULATIONS! Starting with the study of sound is a bold first step, as most people jump into recording without understanding anything at all about the sounds that they wish to work with. You're joining one of a select few who will be able to make high level recordings because you actually took the time to learn how sound works in the recording environment.

Why learn about the basics of sound?

The basics of audio are the fundamental principles of what make up sound. When you understand these basics, you will learn to make better decisions when recording, mixing or designing your studio.

Understanding the basics of audio helps eliminate some of the guesswork that comes when you are recording and mixing. Most great productions happen by design, not by chance. When great performances occur they are usually a solid combination of thinking and the actions behind them that produce classic results.

Whether you're new to recording, or have been recording for a while, I hope you enjoy accompanying me on this journey to gain more insight into your passion, THANK YOU and welcome!

Before we get into the meat of the discussion, let me first tell you a little about myself and my background.

I have a home studio which I call "Music In Your Life Studios" in a small town in New Hampshire. While I never really aimed to make it to the "big time" I do have extensive experience working with music and sound production and sound recording. I am sure many of you may have similar stories, well....here's mine:

Right after College, I spent several years in a couple of different a bands that played in clubs in and around Boston. (Don't worry you've never heard of either one of them.) The city clubs had their own sound systems and sound engineers, so all we had to do was set up and play. While in Boston, I got my first taste of studio recording as our band also made demo recordings in two different area studios.

While we did get some minor notoriety and some sparse airplay on the radio, the real take away was that I was really fascinated by the recording process and making recordings. Ultimately, after a few years of learning how competitive the music business was, I decided I wanted to move back closer to our family's home in New Hampshire. I changed my goal to play in bands only for fun, and to have my own home studio. I took a course in Audio Recording, and graduated as an honor student.

At the same time, I found a way to make a living combining my interests in music with my interests in sound production. I had been a DJ at my College radio station all 4 years of College, and so plagued the local commercial radio station until they hired me. Over the next few years I began to assemble the first vestiges of a home studio beginning with first a four track cassette recorder, and then graduating to 8 track reel to reel. I then moved on to 16 track Digital, and finally to the unlimited tracks that can now be had through modern recording software. (I started with Pro

Tools LE, and now use Cakewalks' Sonar.) I also gained a ton of insight into the mechanics of sound and recording, both working at the radio station, and in my home studio.

Meanwhile I was still hacking around playing in a couple of garage bands-one big difference- was when we were playing gigs around rural New Hampshire and Vermont we had to do our own audio. SO naturally I became the sound engineer for the band, working sound at the same time as playing, which as anyone who has done it knows, can be quite a trick.

One of the opportunities our band had at the time was to play in a local Battle of the Bands competition. But, in order to participate, we had to have a CD in order to enter. At that time, I was in no position to be able to pull off a professional grade recording, so off we trekked to a local recording studio that had done extensive work for professional broadcast. Once again, I got to spend a fair amount of time in a pro studio learning and watching how everything from laying down tracks to editing to mix down all worked. I continued to be fascinated.....

Ultimately the late night schlepping of equipment, low pay, cigarette inhalation, and personal dynamics of working with people who had changing priorities, put more focus on recording things at home. I did spend a couple of years playing solo gigs and doing open mikes, but that wasn't as much fun as making my own recordings. I also made one more foray into a pro studio recording and released a single of an original song called "Miss New Hampshire" just for fun. That recording was released through CD Baby (a service some of you may already be familiar with), I later partnered with them to become a ****Certified Home Studio Partner*****

There is still one more twist to this story, and then I swear...I'll wrap it up......! After running a successful on-line business selling music instruction materials, I eventually got into to giving music lessons to students on guitar and drums. The on-line business was soon cannibalized by former customers who became imitators, and then the big dog

....Amazon .com moved in-I had to make another shift. I moved into the world of education, and taught music at a local elementary school as a supplement to giving lessons. I also worked as a part-time recruiter at the local Community College, which eventually parlayed itself into a full time gig in the College's Continuing Education Department. While working in Continuing Education, I developed and taught a number of music and recording related course. I also taught business classes on-line for College Credit as well as providing independent studies for a couple of students-as the College did not have a music program.

All of this combined experience is what has brought me here today. Now that you know my story, it is my proud honor to share some of the knowledge that I have gained over time with you-so that you can reach for your dreams, expand your hobby, or just plain have fun learning about something you love! Let's move on and begin to learn more about sound....

Chapter One: How Do We Define Sound?

Our first step is to examine what sound is all about. Once we have a broad definition of what sound is, then we can look at how it relates to how our hearing interprets the sound we hear. In this chapter, we will define what sound is, and what sound waves are so we can better understand how to manage them. If we think of ourselves as engineers who are trying to capture the best sound, then the better we understand our subject, the unruly sound wave, the better will be our best chance at success!

Sound can be explained as a disturbance of molecules. These molecules can be air molecules or the molecules of solid objects. When anything happens that makes these molecules vibrate, you get a disturbance....a disturbance which we call sound. Stated simply: sound is produced by moving air.

When a disturbance happens the molecules get squashed together and they shoot off in all directions. These disturbed molecules bump into each other and spread out in compressed waves. They leave an area where there are less molecules behind them. Unless the disturbance is sustained, the particles eventually return to their original state. Air is the type of elastic medium that is needed for sound to exist.

Because air is very elastic, it's also very easy to disturb. A wall is much more rigid but it does have some elasticity so it can also transmit sound. If you hit a wall with a hammer the vibration will travel more quickly than air because the molecules are closer together but it disburses much faster because the material is much more rigid.

One of the most fundamental basics of audio is what is known as the propagation of sound in a space. We call this acoustics, which is all about the science of sound. These principles are used to design recording spaces, control rooms, concert halls, speakers, amplifiers and sound systems all with the purpose of making a balanced and pleasing listening environment. The design of musical instruments and how they project in an acoustic space play a huge role in the choice and placement of microphones that best capture the essence of a given instrument.

How you manage and control the acoustic space, the instrument, and the microphones that capture them, are the most important decisions to be made when recording. Understanding these basic principles, allows you make the best decisions.

Sound waves:

Sound waves are very similar to water waves. If you toss a rock into a body of water, it disrupts the calm of the water. The impact of the rock creates waves as new energy is introduced into the water which creates waves. The stone exerts its weight affecting the surface of the water, causing waves to spread outwards.

Looking at it another way: If you think of an ocean wave, the start of a wave's cycle is the beginning of a wave, continuing with a trough below the water line, and ends with the beginning of the next wave. The difference is that sound waves radiate in all directions, not just on a level surface the way ocean waves do. This is why tossing a rock into a pool of water is a better analogy. Sound waves, like water waves, repeat consecutively with later waves getting weaker and weaker over the course of time. Both water and air waves possess crests and troughs which represent levels of greater or lesser air pressure.

Let's look at this concept from the standpoint of sound emanating from a musical instrument. If we pick a guitar string, the body of the guitar vibrates and produces sound waves as a result of that vibration. Here, instead of the rock disrupting the water, it is the motion of the guitar string vibrating that causes the disruption of air molecules. This vibration sends waves through the air that behave just like the water waves we referenced in our previous example. Our ears detect the variations in air pressure levels and that is what translates as sound to our brain.

It is important to realize that the changes in pressure caused by moving molecules happen at different rates and speeds. What this means is that every different sound is defined by how fast a sound wave travels through its cycle from peak to valley. This is what we recognize as "pitch." Pitch is how high or low a musical note is in terms of is amplitude (how loud a sound is) and its frequency. We define frequency as how quickly a sound wave moves through its cycle. If we use a piano as an example, higher pitches are further to the right of the 88 keys, and lower pitches are to the left of the piano. So as we move from the lowest piano note to the highest we move from left to right.

Summary:

The most important takeaway here is to understand what a sound wave is, and what it looks like. We compared a sound wave to an ocean wave. Sure, we all understand what an ocean wave looks like and how it rises, fades, and then rises again. But how is an ocean wave different from a sound wave? This is the most crucial point to understand from this section!

A sound wave is different because instead of just going back and forth in one direction like a wave you would see at the beach watching the tide, a sound wave disperses in every direction! You can view a wave at the beach in one dimension only-in and out and in and out-in a wide panorama from one side to the other. But a sound wave is circular! It disperses in every direction -not just towards you or away from you, but in every direction at once!

To get this, think about going outside to call your dog or cat. You can yell in one direction, but the fact of the matter the sound doesn't just go straight ahead of you like an ocean wave coming out of your mouth. It goes around you…. it goes in front of you….. it goes to the left….. it goes out the right. Granted it is the loudest in the direction you are shouting, but I can guarantee you that some of that sound goes all around you even behind you a bit.

You are casting sound in every direction when you shout, not just in a single line directly ahead of you. If you shout loud enough, your neighbors can probably attest to that!

Chapter Two: Graphs, Frequency, and Amplitude

Graphs are a great way to create a visual representation of how one element changes in relation to another. Some graphs are used to illustrate both positive and negative values, and as you will see, this is often the case when we use graphs to represent sound waves.

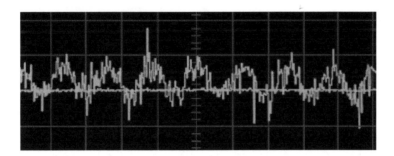

In the graph above, the vertical line represents the amplitude of the sound wave, and the horizontal line represents the frequency. We will be discussing both amplitude and frequency as we next discuss the main characteristics of a sound wave which are:

1) Amplitude
2) Frequency
3) Velocity
4) Wavelength
5) Phase
6) Harmonics
7) Envelope

Amplitude = Loudness

The first characteristic of sound we are going to be discussing is amplitude. Amplitude describes the loudness or softness of any sound that we hear. In our hearing there are limits on the loudest and softest sounds we can pick up on. The amplitude of a sound wave is the height or depth above or below what we call the zero line. The zero line is the point at which there is no measurable sound. It would appear as a flat line on audio graph. Amplitude is also commonly referred to as level, volume, or sound pressure level (spl.)

Amplitude is important to be aware of; as too much or too little sound will affect the quality of the recording you are trying to produce. By the end of this chapter you will have a better understanding of how amplitude affects our ability to effectively capture and reproduce sound.

Normal atmospheric pressure is the level of a sound wave when it is at zero height on a graph. The amplitude of a sound wave is measured as the vertical distance from zero to either the top (also known as the crest) or the bottom (also known as the trough). From this value, the ear evaluates and recognizes the volume of the sound wave. In other words-how loud or soft a given sound is.

If we strum or pick a guitar loudly, the movement of its strings is measurably greater than if it were lightly picked or strummed. In the case of the harder strum or pick, taller sound waves would be produced. This louder sound-which in engineering terms we would call: "increased amplitude" is recognized by the ear in terms of the amount of airwave pressure it recognizes. The brain is sensitive to the signal sent from the ear and interprets that signal to be understood in terms of volume.

We call the limits of human hearing by specific terms. The lowest sounds we can hear we call the threshold of hearing and the highest we call the threshold of pain. The measurement used for loudness-which we now call amplitude-is sound pressure level which is measured with the decibel scale. 0dB SPL is complete quiet, the loudest sound we are able to perceive accurately is about 120 dB SPL.

We can hear at levels louder than 120 dB SPL, but this amount of sound over saturates our hearing and causes distortion that can permanently damage our hearing. 135dB SPL is considered the threshold of pain. 150 dB SPL would cause permanent deafening.

In our next chapter, we'll learn about another fundamental characteristic of sound waves, frequency. You will see how the frequency of a wave determines how high or low the pitch of a sound is, and how it different frequency ranges affect what the listener hears.

Frequency

In this chapter we'll be discussing how the pitch, or how high or low a sound is in order to understand how we can mix different pitches together to make the best recording. By the end of this chapter you'll have a better idea of how to assemble all the different pieces of the audio puzzle into a mix that fits together nicely.

The next factor that the ear senses after a sound wave's amplitude is its frequency. Frequency is the number of times per second that it takes a sound wave complete a full cycle. (Frequency is measured in cycles per second.) A cycle is measured from the start of one wave to the beginning of the next wave. One complete cycle is the span from crest to crest, trough to trough, or any other two identical places on the curve of a sound wave. Measured in cycles per second, frequency units are known as hertz (Hz). Our brain interprets these sounds in terms of what is known as- pitch-the highness or lowness of musical or other tones.

A sound wave that has a frequency of 100 Hz, is a wave that completes its cycle one hundred times every second. For reference, 100 Hz would be a very low note. On the other end of the spectrum, a wave with a frequency of 10,000 Hz would produce a very high note. This wave completes its cycle ten thousand times every second.

One way to illustrate this is by thinking of a musical instrument. In this case, let's use a guitar. Imagine on our guitar that there's two guitar strings of equal length and tension. But if you notice, on a guitar, not all strings are of equal thickness:

Note that one of the strings is roughly twice as thick as the other. When the thicker string is picked, it starts moving air molecules, and moves about twice as much of the surrounding air as the amount of air moved when the thinner string is picked, because it is bigger. As a result of this, the thicker string vibrates about half as fast as the thinner string because it gets more resistance from the air. It vibrates at a slower speed: which means that it produces fewer cycles per second. Fewer cycles per second means that it produces a lower tone.

The total range from lowest to highest frequency in audio waves is called the frequency range or the frequency spectrum. The average human ear can detect sounds around 16 cycles per second for the extremely low sounds, rising to about 16,000 cycles per second for the ultra-highs. This range is normally written: 16Hz to 16kHz (k for kilo, denoting a multiple of 1,000.) This defines the lowest bass frequencies and highest treble frequencies we can perceive.

In reality, most people do not have the capability to perceive sound at this full range. Nor do most need to. The human voice covers a range that is well within those limits. These are the frequencies we are most sensitive to because they define our ability to communicate through the spoken word or sound.

People who work with music and recording and really train their ears can keep this extended frequency response as long as they don't abuse their hearing. If subjected to loud or hurtful volumes on a consistent basis, those capabilities can be permanently lost. I'm afraid after playing in bands all those years that my range of hearing has diminished somewhat- but overall (and to my own amazement) I can still hear pretty well!

As we begin to learn more about the characteristics of sound waves-our next journey is to explore the speed of sound which we call: velocity!

Most of us are familiar with the term "velocity," a term we mostly recognize as a synonym for speed. As it pertains to sound, we have a different definition. Velocity is how long it takes one cycle of a wave to travel in one second through any given medium. Water waves, for example travel through water; and their waves are tracked according to how fast they cycle in terms of troughs and peaks as they travel through water. For sound waves, the medium is typically air molecules. The wave velocity of a sound wave is determined by how long it takes for one cycle of a waveform will travel a certain distance. Sound waves have been typically measured as traveling through air at approximately 1130 feet per second.

There is a simple equation from which we can calculate the velocity, frequency, or wavelength of any sound wave:

(V) Velocity = wavelength x frequency (WxF)
(W) Wavelength= velocity/ frequency (V/F)
(F) Frequency= velocity/wavelength (V/W)

Example: What is the wavelength of a wave which has a frequency of 565 cycles per second (565 Hz)?
Answer: 2 feet.   (Using the formula W=V/F.........W=1130/565=2)

Wavelength

Let's talk a little bit about wavelength. Wavelength is probably one of the elements of a sound wave that is more technical or scientific. But it would be remiss of me not to discuss it. If you're not into the science of sound waves, just bear with me for a couple of minutes. You may never use this knowledge specifically when recording audio, but it will at least make you more familiar with what a sound wave might look like in visual form. You will find as you work with audio recording that there are many opportunities for seeing visual representations of sound waves, so it will be good for you to at least understand how we can define what a sound wave visually looks like.

So how do we define Wavelength? A Wavelength is measured by the distance of a cycle, from one point on a wave curve to the next point of the same height. You should be aware that wavelength increases as the frequency decreases so how far you are from the sound source is an important factor. The key takeaway here is that lower frequencies have longer wavelengths than higher frequencies.

A given sound wave itself can travel a great distance, but that doesn't necessarily mean that the actual particles of the sound wave have moved very far. The way that sound waves work is that the air in one spot is compressed by the sound source. This compresses the air next to it, and it

17

then returns to its original position. This is what we mean when we characterize sound as traveling in a "compression wave." The location of the compression moves at the speed of sound, but the air molecules themselves do not move and travel with the wave. They only move to the extent that they are pushed together and then they release again to return to their original spacing as the wave passes. They stay in this original position until another wave comes along.

Wavelength and Speed of Sound

Wavelength and the speed of sound are audio terms that are depend on each other. The length of a given frequency wave is dependent on the speed at which the sound wave travels. The speed at which sound travels is also affected by the temperature where the sound wave is occurs.

Lower frequencies have longer wavelengths. Higher frequencies have shorter wavelengths. This is determined by some simple math. Measure how far sound travels in 1 second and divide that distance by the number of cycles that occur in that same second.

Sound travels at a rate of 1130 feet per second at 70 degrees Fahrenheit. If you want to know the length of a 100 hertz sound wave, divide 100 into 1130 and you will get 11.3 feet. That is the distance it takes for a 100 hertz waveform to complete one compression and rarefaction cycle.

You can also use the same math to find what frequency is 10 feet long by dividing 10 feet into the speed of sound. 1130 divided by 10 equals 113 Hertz. This basic math is very important to the physical design of recording studios and the acoustic materials that are used to control those frequencies in a recording space. You may find yourself more interested in these types of details if you wish to get deeper into the design and engineering of physical space to maximize the quality of sound in a given environment.

Now that we have had the chance to get a better look at what sound waves look like, and how they vary in length, in our next chapter we will be learning about another important aspect of sound waves, phase. Phase is important to learn about, because it emphasizes why we must be careful about where and how we place our microphones when we are recording more than one instrument at a time!

Chapter Four: Phase

Understanding Phase and what phase cancellation is all about is integral to understanding the recording process. It is such a large consideration that you will hear about it many times before this narrative has concluded. Phase issues are a result of live sound issues caused by the use of multiple microphones. By the end of this chapter, you will learn why it is important to pay attention to how and where you set your microphones up when you are planning a recording.

Remember, the cycle of a wave can begin at any point on the wave form, either above or below the zero line. The best way to understand a given wave is to break it down into 360 degrees in order to be able to identify different points along the path of each cycle.

If two sound waves have the same amplitude, frequency, and shape, they are considered to be "out of phase" with each other if they reach their peaks at different times. The two waves will remain "in phase" with each other regardless of their amplitude, if they reach their peaks at the same time. So think of two rainbows. If the rainbows appear as a double rainbow, with the peaks in the same place that would be the visual representation of two in phase sound waves (even though one is bigger than the other.) But, if there were two rainbows were skewed, and had peaks in different places, then they would look visually like out of phase sound waves.

Let's imagine that two different sound waves, are for all intents and purposes the same. They have identical shapes, frequencies, and amplitudes. If they reach their peaks at different times, they would be "out of phase with each other." It doesn't matter if the sound waves have different heights (loudness, or amplitude), if they reach their peaks at the same time, they would be considered to be "in phase" with each other.

So when is a sound wave considered to be "out of phase?" Anytime those peaks don't match up. In fact the most out of phase condition occurs when one cycle of a sound wave begins right when another sound wave reached halfway point of its cycle. Think of the McDonald's "Golden Arches." If you were to slide the right arch into the middle of the first arch, that would be the visual equivalent of a wave that was its most out of phase position. In this case the waves are said to be 180 degrees out of phase with each other, and if the two waves are combined, they will completely cancel out one another resulting in absolutely no sound.

This same "phase" phenomenon, doesn't just apply to sound waves, it also affects electrical waves as well. Why do I mention this? When it comes to recording, microphones are one of our most important tools. Remember, the microphone is responsible for converting acoustical sound into electrical waves.) Electrical phase cancellation happens when signals of opposite polarity and equal amplitude are combined.

Phase cancellation is especially noticeable when two or more microphones are placed close to one another. If the distance from one mic to a given source of sound reaches a positive peak of a sound wave reaches that mic at the same time that the negative peak of the same sound wave reaches another mic, phase cancellation will occur if the two signals are combined. Remember that two separate mics are working with two completely different signals. Even if the mics are in close proximity there may be enough difference in sound waves to begin to cause phase cancellation, even if they are close to the same distance from the sound source.

On its own, each mic will sound fine, but if the two signals are combined there is serious deformation in the sonic quality. It is usually noticeable as a loss of critical mid-range frequencies, the signal will have a thin hollow sound which is evidence of phase cancellation. In this case the two waveforms are interfering with each other in a destructive manner, which causes this phenomenon. Be aware that waveforms also can interfere with each other constructively, when signals are combined from more than one microphone it can also be a nice sound enhancement-as long as you are aware of the dangers of phase cancellation-it can be an effective tool to combine signals.

There are also instances where adding frequencies by amplitude is actually considered constructive. But in this case it is considered to be positive, even though sonic deformation occurs, but this time, these frequencies become exaggerated. This is why many vocal and instrument tracks are doubled, tripled, and some cases even more than that. It makes the original tracks stronger, and more prominent. You may have heard this described as" building a wall of sound."

A simple copy and paste is not as effective as a separate performance or take-because there are subtle nuances in each performance, it allows them to breathe a little bit and extra nuance to a performance. Human space, slight error, and alteration is a positive thing to most recordings. It keeps recordings from sounding mechanical or overproduced. (Don't even talk to me about auto-tune!)

Phase cancellation is most notable when the sound from two microphones that are out of, are sent to the left and right speakers through the mixing console in the control room. The mix will sound fine in stereo, but if you pan the signals to a central point between the speakers, or if you switch the system to mono, the sound will almost completely disappear because the sound waves have interfered with one another.

Up to this point, we have only been looking at single waveforms. Fact of the matter though, when it comes to recording, we usually deal with complex waveforms where phase cancellation is not quite so apparent. Though the polarities of the waveforms (plus or minus) are often opposite at any given time, it is unusual for their amplitudes to be the same, so the sonic deformation, although present, is less obvious.

Whenever signals follow different paths to the same point, there is a very high probability that phase cancellation will happen if the signals from the two paths are put together. This is one reason we try to avoid leakage between instruments when recording. If there is more than one microphone being used during a live recording you can run into issues with phase cancellation. The individual mics may sound fine, but if more than one signal is combined at the mixing point, the complete sound may be imperfect.

This is a result of phase cancellation because the sound waves have reached each mic at different points in their cycle. Since a "leaking" sound wave has farther to travel, it will reach any additional mics at a different point in their cycle. This condition leads to cancellation of some frequencies resulting in poor sound quality.

Coming Up we'll be discussing details on things to beware as we study using multiple microphones to capture sound.

Using Multiple Microphones To Capture Sound.

When several instruments are recorded simultaneously, each having its own microphone, some of the sound from one instrument may stray into the microphones that are directed at other instruments. This is called leakage or cross-bleed and is something we definitely want to watch out for. Separation is the term we use to describe the degree to which these undesirable effects are minimized. One method of improving separation is by physically inserting acoustic screens (also known as "baffles") between each instrument. You can also record separate instruments or vocals at different times, so that you have fewer open mics going.

Some performers like playing together to capture that "live" feel when they record in the studio, so that is the time to be most aware of phase cancellation, and sound leakage from instrument to another. You almost always see vocals recorded in an isolation booth (sometimes shortened to be called just "iso") in order to maintain separation. Usually iso booths have a window in them so that the singer can still interact with the performers if they are cutting tracks live. Vocals are usually the lead instrument, so you definitely want to ensure the best possible sound when recording them!

The alternative is to record separate tracks for playing each different sound. Performers then record their individual parts one at a time, while they listen to the other part(s) through headphones. This has become more common. Although it may reduce some of the interaction between performers, a good performance usually maintains its energy if the individual puts their full vibe into their playing, and the producer makes sure that they capture the best possible take.

Many times performers will put in a scratch track (usually a quick vocal) so they can keep track of where they are at in the performance, and make sure their parts land in the right place in the song. There is always at least one instrument which has to go first, and you build around it. My experience is that wherever the song came from is the best place to start. For example if the song was written on an acoustic guitar, then begin with that as a scratch track along with a scratch vocal. Just make sure, whatever you do that the initial recording matches exactly what you want the song to do. Once you have a glitch-especially a rhythmic one, you will be stuck with that glitch forever unless you correct it at the get go.

There are other techniques such as overdubbing and "comping" which are more in depth than what we will be discussing here. But suffice it to say that recording tracks one at a time provides the best possible opportunity for capturing the cleanest sound. There are times when a couple of instruments will lay down their tracks a t the same time to maintain that live energy that comes from interaction. That is often the case with Bass and drums. Sometimes the rhythm section will put down their parts together.

Speaking of drums, I'll close on this note. If you are recording an acoustic drum set-you will never get away from having to be sensitive about mic placement. Drums require multiple mics to capture the best representation of their sound, so being aware of placement and phase cancellation will be important especially in this setting. The only way around this is if you are using triggers on the drums which will send an electronic signal in place of a microphone. But cymbals always need to be recorded live, so that doesn't completely eliminate the possibility of phase cancellation, since you will need more than one mic to accurately capture the full sound of the cymbals.

The exception of course is if you are using a drum machine, or are using loops, or electronic drums. In those cases the sounds are reproduced without using any acoustic sounds, so there is no need for any mixing at all in those cases.

I hope you can see the importance and relevance of these different characteristics of sound waves, as we discuss how they affect sound recording. Phase is an especially important consideration, as once you are stuck with phase in your system, it is difficult to remove. It's not the type of issue that lends itself to an easy "fix in the mix."

Stay tuned as next chapter we learn about another characteristic of sound waves that can affect the sound of your recording: Harmonics! We'll explore all about overtones, and complementary sounds like Octave tones that also live in the dynamic range of the sounds we are recording. They too can make a difference to how good your recording ultimately sounds.

Chapter Five: Harmonics

In this chapter we're going to learn about Harmonics. We' will see why it is important to maintain flat frequency response in our system in order to not interfere with the natural sounds that are produced by musical instruments. Our goal again is to capture the best possible sound, so let's look a little more about why being aware of harmonics and understanding them can help us make better recordings.

Any musical instrument have ten or more harmonic frequencies that are related to its fundamental frequency. They're kind of like built-in harmony groups, some of them sound harmonious, and some sound dissonant.

The way that we discern which musical instrument is playing which particular sound is very much distinguished by the presence and ratios of harmonics. It is the presence of these harmonics which make one sound have a much different sound from another, even if they both have the same basic frequency.

Harmonic frequencies are usually exact multiples of what we call the fundamental frequency. The fundamental frequency is also often referred to as the first harmonic. For Example, if we define 1,000 Hz as a fundamental frequency, its second harmonic would be 2,000 Hz, and its third harmonic would be 3,000Hz, and so on. Harmonics are divided into two groups: even multiples give even harmonics, while odd multiples give odd harmonics.

Fundamental	Even Harmonic	Odd Harmonic
1,000 Hz	2,000 Hz	3,000 Hz
	4,000 Hz	5,000 Hz
	6,000 Hz	7,000 Hz
	8,000 Hz	9,000 Hz

Our ears particularly notice those harmonics that have a frequency ratio of 2:1 . This ratio particularly resonates with our hearing as it is the basis of the musical octave.

Here's an example: For our purposes let's begin with the frequency of a concert A note. A "concert A" is 440 Hz and the ear hears 880 Hz as the next note higher to "concert A" which is most like "concert A". This 880 Hz note is said to be one octave higher than 440 Hz. The next highest note to have similar sounding characteristics is 1760 Hz, which is two octaves above the original or fundamental note.

The human ear does not respond to all frequencies of waves. Its range spans about 10 octaves which in terms of frequency is 16 to 16,000 Hz.

First Octave	16 to 32 Hz
Second Octave	32-64 Hz
Third Octave	64 to 128 Hz
Fourth Octave	128 to 256 Hz
Fifth Octave	256 to 512 Hz
Sixth Octave	512-1028 Hz
Seventh Octave	1028 to 2048 Hz
Eighth Octave	2048 to 4096 Hz
Ninth Octave	4096 to 8192 Hz
Tenth Octave	8192 to 16,394 Hz

Because the waveform of a musical instrument has these harmonics of different amplitudes, it bears little resemblance to the shape of a simple single frequency sine wave. Sine waves do not generate harmonics, they are what defines a single tone.

The complex waveforms of musical instruments are not usually of a repetitive nature and it is difficult to divide them into cycles or pinpoint their frequency by looking at the wave shape. For example, the human voice creates energy at many different frequencies simultaneously. It is not easy to measure frequencies in a complex wave form, however, such a waveform merely consists of multiple combinations of simple wave forms of differing frequencies, amplitudes, and phases. On reaching the ear it separates the complex waveforms into their simple sine wave equivalents before transmitting them to the brain. So the brain interprets these complex sounds as if they were a single unified sound.

The harmonic content that the brains interprets this sound is what characterizes the characteristic sound of an instrument. We call this distinctive sound "timbre." As defined by Merriam Webster's dictionary, timbre is "the quality of the sound made by a particular voice or musical instrument."

This helps explain why the frequency response of microphones, amplifiers and speakers should be as flat as possible. We don't anything that is not part of the instrument itself to alter its sound, because we do not want to alter the relative levels of the harmonics of any signal. If the frequency response is not flat-then the timbre of the instrument will change. Equalizers are pieces of equipment that can be used to alter the timbre of any sound.

To summarize, the importance of harmonics are that they help define an instrument's sound. When you alter an instrument's sound with equalization you could be shifting it away from some of its resonant qualities, so it is important not to over-equalize a given instrument (unless you are doing that on purpose to create a unique effect.)

The real point of emphasis here is that many different timbres (distinctive instruments sounds) live within a given frequency range. If they are all piled up in one area of a given frequency range they can make your mix sound muddy and lifeless. It can be really hard to get any particular instrument to stick out in a mix where there is a ton of sound in a given Hz range. You want to be especially careful not to bury vocals in a muddy mix!

One of the secrets that audio engineers use to open up the frequency spectrum is to shift a given instrument further towards the left or right of the stereo image. This is known as panning. I am sure if you listen to enough music, you hear times when a guitar-especially a lead guitar is panned hard to the right or left. That opens up more of the middle of the spectrum for the vocals. It is not unusual to hear a rhythm guitar panned hard right and a lead guitar, or even a guitar with a different tone panned hard left at the same time. You can move instruments to different sides of the stereo image in varying degrees to create space for other instruments in the mix. Usually lead vocals are right in the middle. Sometimes bass and bass drum are put there too, because they are usually low enough in frequency that they won't interfere with vocals.

There's one more characteristic for sound waves to cover: Envelope. In our next chapter, we will take a look at how Envelope describes the overall shape of the waveform of a musical instrument.

Chapter Six: Envelope

Let's explore one more final element of sound : Envelope. There is one distinct characteristic of sound that describes the overall shape of a waveform of a musical instrument. That characteristic is what we refer to as "Envelope."

 By learning about a waveform's envelope we can understand why it important to monitor sound waves so that we know the exact right time to fade them in or out, or even to split or cut them if they need to be edited. Envelope also gives us the basis for understanding how compressors and limiters affect waveforms, which we'll investigate shortly.

It is not just harmonic content that tells us which particular instrument is producing a certain note. Every note produces its own envelope which works in combination with harmonic content that makes it unique. Remember, envelope describes the overall shape of the waveform of a musical instrument including its changes in loudness from the beginning to the end of the sound of each note. Envelope is made up of three distinct sections which relate to the beginning, middle and end of the waveform: Attack, Sustain, and Delay.

Let's take a quick look at how some of the characteristics of envelope define sound: Envelopes which possess a short attack and fast initial decay will sound percussive, whereas slow attacks and slower decays give rise to softer, more even sounds.

By using certain pieces of studio equipment (or plug-ins in the case of software programs) known as compressors, limiters and expanders, we can modify the envelope of an instrument without affecting its timbre. Compressors and limiters are specialized amplifiers used to reduce dynamic range — the span between the softest and loudest sounds. The use of compressors can make recordings and live mixes sound more polished by controlling maximum levels and maintaining higher average loudness. Additionally, many compressors — both hardware and software — will have a signature sound that can be used to inject an amazing array of coloration and tone into otherwise lifeless tracks.

Compression can also be used to subtly massage a track to make it more natural sounding and intelligible without adding distortion, resulting in a song that's more "comfortable" to listen to. Alternately, over-compressing your music can really squeeze the life out of it. We won't get into the specifics of using a compressor or limiter here. Our focus is on understanding the characteristic of sound known as envelope, which gives us the fundamental science behind how compressors and limiters affect sound waves.

Next, we'll take a quick review and summary of all of the different characteristics of sound. Then we'll dig more deeply into amplitude specifically. The loudness of sound has some important implications as it relates to recording, so it is worth spending a little bit more time on that subject specifically.

Chapter Seven: AMPLITUDE: The Loudness of Sound

As we begin to translate our understanding of sound and sound waves into practical action. We now turn our attention to one of the most important qualities when it comes to recording: The Loudness of Sound.

The Decibel:

Sound produces waves by expanding and contracting the air molecules near the sound source. As we have learned, this disturbance in air molecules is discernable by the human ear. These waves cause the air pressure to become higher or lower than normal atmospheric pressure. The ear recognizes these pressure variations and translates them into sound. As The ear operates over an extremely wide range, being able to respond to all sounds whose amplitude lies within a ratio of one thousand billion to one.. (1,000,000,000,000:1).

So how do we measure those changes in sound pressure? With a unit known as a "decibel." The decibel is a unit of measurement for both acoustical and electrical sound levels. It expresses the ratio between the strengths of two sound levels.

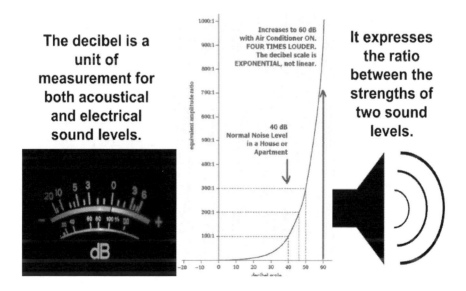

The decibel is a unit of measurement for both acoustical and electrical sound levels.

It expresses the ratio between the strengths of two sound levels.

If you were close to the engine of a Boeing 747 jet as it took off, the acoustical noise level would reach about 150 decibels (dB), which is equivalent to 10 thousand billion times louder than the threshold of hearing. Because the ear is so incredibly sensitive to extreme variations of high and low levels, these astronomical figures become quite unmanageable, so they are scaled down into smaller, but still related numbers. To do this, the monster numbers are scaled down through the use of mathematical logarithms.

The logarithm of a number is that power to which 10 must be raised to equal the number. So, if our jet aircraft produces a sound level which is 10,000,000,000,000 times more intense than the threshold of hearing, that figure can be represented by its logarithmic equivalent which is 10^15 (or 150 dB), which of course, is a much less cumbersome number to work with.

Remember, the dB measuring system does not represent tangible units such as inches, ounces, or minutes, it is only the expression of the ratio of two powers. Absolute levels can only be determined if a reference level is chosen for one of these powers. Therefore, in acoustical sound measurements, 0dB is fixed at the threshold of hearing. This is the lowest sound pressure level (spl) that an average human ear can detect ; it is not, as one might expect, absolute silence, nor is it atmospheric pressure

A 2:1 ratio (twice as much power) is equivalent to a 3dB difference.-

Thus, if a certain sound is measured to be 50 dB above the level of the threshold of hearing, for this sound to be doubled in volume, the dB equivalent would be 53dB (not 100dB). As we will explore later, this type of increase is in step with the manner in which our ears actually perceive volume changes.

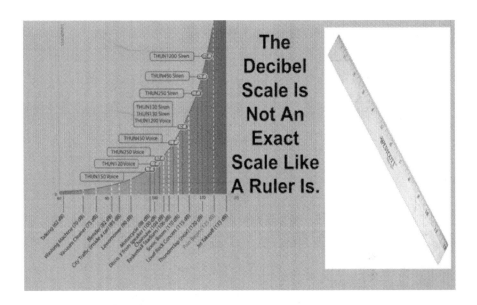

The system I just described was developed to measure <u>acoustical power</u>. Decibels are also used to measure the <u>electrical power</u> of sound after it has been converted from acoustical energy by the microphone. So be aware that acoustical power and electrical power are two entirely different things.

The method of calculation for electrical power is the same as acoustical power, but the zero reference level is different. In a studio, the reference is not the threshold of hearing, but it is fixed as being the voltage found in a typical recording console. In this way, <u>electrical</u> dB levels can be expressed and related to each other. We can then compare other voltages as a ratio to this level, and note that they are either above or below our zero reference.

So now you should understand what decibels are, and why most sound meters are calibrated the way they are.

Chapter Eight: Electrical Sound Waves

Let's now focus our attention specifically on electrical sound waves. In order to be able to know how to contain electrical signals within the limits and capacity of your recording equipment, it is important to learn about the strengths of electrical signals. By the end of this chapter, you will know more about the common methods of measuring the voltage strength of an electrical signal, and what happens if you don't pay attention to how it affects your equipment.

As soon as an acoustical wave has been picked up by a microphone, it is converted into an electrical wave which possesses similar rising and falling patterns (crests and troughs) as an acoustical sound wave. However, once a signal becomes electrified, the increases and decreases in level are measured in voltages rather than pressure differentials.

Electrical wave peaks possess far more voltage than their troughs. Time (frequency in cycles per second) is still an important consideration. There are an infinite number of instantaneous values throughout the cycle of each wave, which means that specific measurements can be determined in a number of ways.

The most common method of measuring the voltage strength of an electrical wave, is known as "peak to peak reading." The second most common method is taking an average reading during one complete wave cycle, which is known as "average signal strength." Average signal strength is measured in RMS volts (root-mean-square) , and is equal to 70.7 % of the peak value. Take a look at this illustration which shows a comparison between the two:

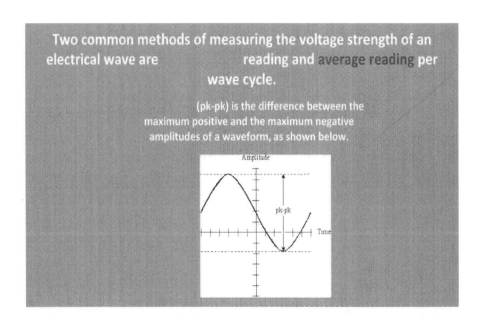

Two common methods of measuring the voltage strength of an electrical wave are _____ reading and average reading per wave cycle.

(pk-pk) is the difference between the maximum positive and the maximum negative amplitudes of a waveform, as shown below.

Sound engineers need to know the strength of electrical signals in order to be able to contain them within the limits and capacity of the recording equipment. The equipment is designed to accept signals within certain predetermined levels. Signals that are too low will not record well and those which are too high will result in overload, distortion, and possibly even seriously damage the equipment.

I'll give you an example. When I was doing sound for our band, I was routing some of our sound through a pair of Bose PA speakers. In a somewhat less than brilliant move, I was also routing the mics from the Bass and the snare drum to these speakers, not really worrying about the voltage coming into them. What I failed to consider was that because of the powerful energy that comes from consistent low tones, one of the speakers blew because the cone was not designed to handle that amount of bass tone. It was a costly lesson, because it cost me a fair amount to replace the cone in that speaker. However, after that I at least knew enough to make sure to send bass tones to equipment that was designed to be able to handle that amount of power.

To summarize: the most important characteristic that we notice in examining electrical waves, as opposed to regular (or acoustical) sound waves-is that we measure electrical voltage instead of sound pressure level. (Which we also refer to as Hertz).

In our next chapter, we'll look in more detail about controlling sound with our recording equipment, beginning with a discussion on setting recording levels. Probably the single most consideration when making a recording is setting recording levels. Once you have recorded something it is very difficult to affect the level of what you have down on your drive.

Chapter Nine: Controlling Sound in the Recording Environment

In this chapter, we'll be talking about the most important considerations that you will want to make when making a recording of any sound.

It is always important to be able to set the highest possible recording level for every sound that is recorded. This way, there is not a whole lot of variance in the sound of what you are recording.

A major source of concern for recording audio engineers lies in the fact that recording devices (including hard drives) and amplifiers have certain limitations in the range of signals which they can accept without producing distortion or unwanted noise. Unlike our ears, which allow us to perceive 100% of all sound, most recording devices can handle only about 50 % of the total range. This is equal to about 60 dB and any signal must be contained within these limits.

Distortion is a sound which almost everybody recognizes. It happens whenever a piece of equipment is worked beyond its limits. Recording mediums become saturated when too much signal is coming into the system and the resulting sound is known as clipping. Loudspeakers make the signal sound muddy and poorly defined when they are overloaded with power. As I shared with you in the last chapter, physical damage can sometimes result when recording equipment is subjected to excessive signal loads.

Our real challenge is that no amount of first aid or magical processing devices can get rid of distortion once it has been recorded. It is therefore of prime importance to know the precise levels of any particular signal so that you can contain it within the limitations of the system. A visual display is the tool we use to monitor signal strength.

Next we'll take an in-depth look at volume unit meters: the monitors which tell us how much signal is actually being recorded. You'll soon see why they are one of the most important tools in helping us to shape our sound correctly.

Chapter Ten: The Loudness of Sound

In this Chapter, we're going to discuss how we monitor and measure the loudness of sound. We do this so that we can set levels as accurately as possible. That way we can limit distortion, outside noise, and produce a sharp clear sound that maximizes its quality as we continue our quest to capture the best possible sound.

By the end of this chapter, you'll know what those level meters on your recording device are and how they can provide you with the most useful information.

There are meters which measure signal strength in a number of different ways. The most convenient indication of signal strength is represented on meters which are called a Volume Unit~ abbreviated as "VU." These meters measure sound strength not in decibels, but in volume units. A Volume Unit meter shows a scale with a 0VU point marked about two thirds of the way across. After that there is a final third beyond which lies a red band indicating possible distortion if the sound level raises enough to make the needle enter this area.

VU meters, however, don't tell the whole story. They only show an average reading, and VU Meters ignore sudden rapid peaks in the signal. This limitation is inherent in their design. If the meter shows a reading of 0 VU, invisible, sudden instantaneous peaks in a signal could be as high as + 15 VU or more above at this point.

Since audio levels are constantly in motion with occasional, sudden peaks, the ear tends to ignore those peaks when evaluating average loudness. VU meters are designed to read an average between peak levels and general program content. The meter is a volume indicator, calibrated in volume units, and visually approximates what the ear perceives. These short term peaks, (also known as "transients"), can exceed the indicated values by as much as 15 VU. Therefore, in a recording console, or tape recorder, the electronics in the signal path following the VU meters are designed to possess enough *headroom* to contain these "transients" without distortion. The area between 0 VU and +15 VU is called 15 VU *headroom.*

Recording systems need to be designed to handle peaks without distortion. Headroom is the term given to the difference in level between normal operating level (0 VU) and the point at which distortion occurs (typically +15 VU in an average system).

While recording, it is crucial to keep the program material as high as possible without distortion, so that the quieter passages, unwanted hiss or other system noise is kept to an absolute minimum. Once recorded, the level of this noise cannot be lowered. However, if the program level is raised to the highest possible level it tends to mask that noise level and it appears to be less. Normal operating level is 0 VU, although if it were known that there were definitely no transient peaks in the signal to cause distortion, a higher operating level could be set and the VU meter could be allowed to safely enter the red zone.

Certain musical instruments, such as the piano, tambourine, and drums, contain high transient peaks of energy levels. Back in the old days of VU meters, when there was an actual needle in the monitor, if the needle swung all the way over to the right hand side retaining pin, and stayed there, it was known as "pinning the meter". You may still hear that statement once in awhile, but the real point is to avoid "peaking the meter" as it now commonly referred to as, because it can be harmful to the device.

One important point: it should be mentioned that the meter readings on a recorder or recording console are not readings of the acoustical sound level from the speakers in your control room. They are a measurement of the electrical power which is passing through the console , after it has been converted from acoustical power into electrical power by a microphone.

Peak Program Meters (PPM) are another type of sound meter. The Peak Program meter , looks pretty much the same as the VU meter. The difference between the two is that PPM's , actually do indicate sudden instantaneous program peaks. These spikes occur so fast that a gradual tail-off of the needle is engineered into the ballistics of the meter so that the movement is not too rapid for the eye to see.

Some engineers prefer PPMs (Peak Program Meters), as they respond more clearly to high transients, which can be damaging to a recording, but more importantly, could actually be damaging to your system. Furthermore, as the PPM is not averaging the program material (like the VU meter), it is correct to read the level in decibels.

There are also meters which use light emitting diodes (LEDs) where the illumination corresponds to the levels. Fast transient peaks register better on LEDs than on the conventional meter which possesses a needle. The ideal visual level indicator would show both the average content and the peak content of a signal; LED lights for the peaks, combined with a VU meter for the average volume. Unfortunately we rarely see this type of combination installed in recording equipment.

The nature of digital systems is such that even the briefest of transient overloads is clearly audible, so neither VU nor PPM metering is suitable. The majority of digital recorders, mixers and converters therefore use true peak-reading meters whose displays are derived from the digital data stream. As these don't rely on analog level-sensing electronics they can be extremely accurate.

Analog meters all have a nominal alignment point — the zero reference — with a bit of headroom above. The idea is that signal peaks are routinely allowed into the first 8dB or so of this headroom, though peaks of +12 dBu will usually start to cause distortion which becomes more and more noticeable with increasing level until clipping occurs, usually at between

18dBu and 22 dBu.

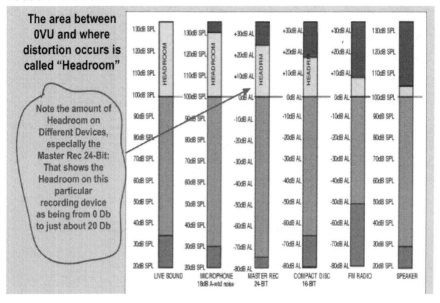

The area between 0VU and where distortion occurs is called "Headroom"

Note the amount of Headroom on Different Devices, especially the Master Rec 24-Bit: That shows the Headroom on this particular recording device as being from 0 Db to just about 20 Db

To recap - we've talked about how we visually measure sound, the different tools we use to measure it, and why it is important to maximize the quality of the sounds we record. In the next chapter, we'll talk about how we hear sound, in order to understand how best to mix sounds of different frequencies so they sound good together.

Chapter Eleven: How we Hear Sound

In this chapter, we're going to talk about How We Hear Sound. Our goal here is to understand how the human ear perceives certain frequencies as being louder than others, even though in reality that may not be the case at all. It is important to know this when you are recording and mixing sounds together, so you can understand why certain frequencies are sometimes emphasized more than others when it comes to the mix down.

Studies indicate that everybody possesses a slightly different hearing response. As we mentioned in the last chapter, most human ears can detect frequencies ranging from about 16 Hz to around 16,000 kHz. People who have subjected themselves to prolonged exposure to high levels of sound, lose hearing first in the upper frequencies and later in the midrange.

We have learned that the frequency range or bandwidths of an instrument or voice are terms used to describe the range between the highest and lowest frequencies of its signal. Our hearing range , the range from 16 Hz to 16 kHz; is equivalent to approximately 10 octaves. We also want to bear in mind that every instrument also contains harmonics which have much higher frequencies.

Any time we are recording multiple sounds that have different frequencies, we want to keep in mind that the human ear does not behave in a perfectly linear fashion. The ear needs progressively greater amounts of sound in order to perceive a linear change in volume. For example, if you listen to a sound which is registering 5VU on a VU meter , in order for the human ear to perceive a doubling in the loudness of this sound, the signal must be boosted to read 15 VU on the meter, and not 10 VU as you might expect. This is the meaning of a non-linear response.

The ear's sensitivity to volume is not constant throughout the entire frequency range. It is most sensitive to midrange frequencies between 2000Hz and 4000Hz, and less sensitive to lower and higher frequencies.

As an example, a 3 kHz sine wave will sound louder than a 10 kHz sine wave, even if both of them are at the same sound pressure level. Similarly, a 100Hz sine wave will also appear to be quieter than a 3 kHz sine wave, if both are of the same spl (sound pressure level).

Our ears get confused by harmonic distortion in sound waves above a certain volume level; they can actually invent harmonics. This is why it's good to mix at lower volume levels. The ear's perception of loudness is not directly proportional over the entire frequency range.

So what we want to remember is that the ear is more sensitive to different frequencies, even though the volume of both may be the same. Let me share with you this example from my own experience which helps illustrate this: I was working as a DJ, doing a wedding at an outdoor wedding. After setting all of my equipment up, I had started playing some background music for the guests to enjoy. Unexpectedly, one of the guests pulled me aside, and asked "what's wrong with the sound system? It's hurting my ears!"

The question took me aback, as I had spent a significant amount of time setting up, and the music was playing just fine. I wrote it off as just some old fuddy-duddy that didn't like loud music, so I turned the volume down just a tad. Of course I slowly worked the sound back up to its original volume again, and even dared to push it just a teensy bit louder. I had set up all of my DJ equipment on the side of an outside tent, and the speakers were inside. So I was monitoring the sound from just outside the tent, without actually walking inside the tent to hear how it sounded. To me, it sounded fine.

Shortly thereafter, another guest approached me, and mentioned the same thing. That the music was hurting their ears! Well, once was odd enough, but a second warranted further investigation. So, I went under the tent, and it became very obvious time what the problem was. All the high frequencies were boosted and everything sounded like tin! Not to mention that it was hurting everyone's ears, because the high frequency pitches were so sensitive to human hearing.

As I looked at my mixing board, I could see that I had accidently hit some of the knobs during set-up, and all the high frequencies were turned way up. No wonder everyone's ears were hurting! I quickly made EQ adjustments, and the sound was great after that. Everyone was happy, and I learned to always check my settings and walk around the venue to listen to the sound before the event begins.

In our next chapter...we'll get into more details about this frequency response difference, so that we can be more aware of which frequencies to boost and which ones to cut when mixing and recording. This will give us more of an edge as we look once again to capture and reproduce the best possible sound!

Chapter Twelve: Frequency Response

In this chapter, we'll get into more details about which frequencies to boost and which ones to cut when mixing and recording and why. By the end of this chapter you will have a firm understanding of a few quirks that are unique to sound as you are preparing your recordings for mix down.

In order to continue our quest to capture and reproduce the best possible sound, we will now explore what are called "The Fletcher-Munson Curves."

Two gentlemen by the names of Fletcher and Munson analyzed the ear's response to different frequencies at different volumes and came up with a graph showing the results. They named the two lines on the graph lines of response and equal loudness contours. If you look at these curves carefully you can get a general understanding of which frequencies appear louder at varying levels of volume.

As you can see, the low frequencies have to be boosted considerably, by as much as 60 dB in some cases, to be perceived equal in level to frequencies at 3.5kHz, when both are actually at the same sound pressure level.
At a high volume of say, 11dB sound pressure level, the levels of 30 Hz and 1 kHz seem much closer.
Remember my story from the last chapter about my DJ experiences? This is the science that explains that phenomenon!

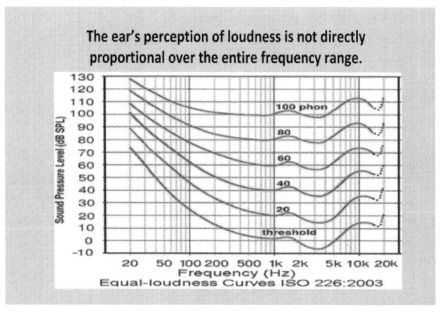

The ear's perception of loudness is not directly proportional over the entire frequency range.

Equal-loudness Curves ISO 226:2003

The curves show the ear's relative sensitivity at different sound pressure levels. Note the ear's increased sensitivity in the 3.5 kHz area.

The implications of this phenomenon cannot be overemphasized. A satisfactory balance of frequencies heard at one level can appear to be totally unbalanced when listened to at another level!

This is why most engineers monitor and mix at moderate, rather than high or low levels. If the recording is played at a quieter level, this approach produces much more accurate sound. Too much bass is generally preferable than too little bass. Most home listening levels average in the 70-85 dB spl range; therefore this would be the optimum level for the engineer to listen while mixing.

To add further to the confusion , the loudness of a tone can also affect the ear's perception of the pitch of that tone. The pitch will decrease as the sound level increases. A 100Hz tone decreases by 10 percent when its spl is increased from 40 to 100 dB. At 500 Hz, this decrease would amount to about 2 percent when comparing the same two volume levels. With this this in mind, it is wiser to tune your instrument at fairly low volumes.

Another idiosyncrasy of human perception happens when two tones lie very close to each other in frequency and both are at about the same volume. The ear will perceive beats equal to the difference between the two tones. For example, the ear hears a tone of 1,000Hz and a tone of 1,020Hz, it will also hear a slow beating tone of 20Hz.

Another point worth mentioning is that combination tones are produced when two loud tones differ by more than 50Hz. The ear senses additional tones equal to both the sum and difference of the two original tones. For example, if we play two loud tones of 1 kHz and 3kHz the ear will perceive a third tone of 2 kHz (3 kHz-1 kHz) and a fourth tone of 4 kHz (3 kHz + 1 kHz). The ear also perceives tones equal to the sum and difference of their respective harmonics.

Finally, one more irregularity of the human ear: a loud sound can mask a softer one. This is most noticeable when the two sounds are close together in frequency. For example, a loud 5 kHz tone can mask a softer 4 kHz tone, yet it will have little effect on a soft 1 kHz tone.

Some of these facts might seem a little difficult to grasp at first, but as you continue learning about recording , you will come across new data which will help reinforce these basic theories and they will make more sense when you get into actual recording situations. These are some things to listen for and be aware of particularly when you get to the mix down stage of a production. You have to constantly listen to instruments in each frequency range, and make sure they are reproduced the way you truly want to hear them.

Usually what I do is mix a recording, burn it to both a CD and to a Wav file. (Not MP3! As MP3 important data taken away from it so you don't get a true representation of sound!). I then listen in different systems at different volumes, my car, my phone, an old home stereo, and of course on my original system. You'd be surprised at how different a mix can sound on a different system.

Many systems have a series of different EQ settings that vary according to what type of music you are listening to. I go through that cycle as well. What I'm looking for is a good blend in any situation, and I often discover something "sticking out" or "missing" that I didn't notice when I was doing the original mix down. If I can find someone else to listen to it, I like doing that too. Manny times other people will notice things that I didn't in the original mix.

Next, we will learn about the importance of flat frequency response, and also how to divide the frequency spectrum up into three major pieces. That will give us a better idea of how to communicate about and manage the sounds we are trying to capture and reproduce.

Chapter 13: Flat Frequency Response

In this chapter we will learn what is meant by the term "Flat frequency Response." We will also be discussing how to divide the frequency spectrum up into three major pieces. That will give you a better idea of how to communicate about and manage the sounds we are trying to capture and reproduce.

A flat frequency response would be created by an instrument which was capable of producing notes of exactly equal volume levels throughout its' entire frequency range. In other words, the amplitude (volume) of its lowest notes must equal the amplitude (volume) of its highest notes, and all that are in between should be the same.

Bear in mind some of the various idiosyncrasies we have talked about when it comes to sound and the human ear. The ear can play tricks on us that make certain frequencies seem louder to us than they actually are. That is why aim to have equipment and monitoring systems that can accurately represent sounds, instead of us making judgements simply based on what we THINK we hear.

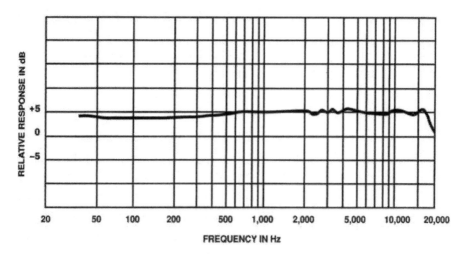

FLAT FREQUENCY RESPONSE

We can see in the figure that the frequency is determined from the horizontal line and the response, or loudness is read from the vertical line. If the output amplitude is the same at all frequencies , the curve would be a flat straight line from right to left, hence the name flat frequency response. It indicates that no frequency is emphasized more or less than any other. If the curve was to rise or dip at any given frequency, we could deduce that that particular frequency has a higher or lower amplitude than the others.

A recording studio strives to produce the flattest possible frequency beginning point. We then will divide the frequency spectrum up into three major pieces. That will give us a better idea of how to communicate about and manage the sounds we are trying to capture and reproduce frequency response at all points in the recording chain, from the microphone through the recorder and amplifier right up to and including the loudspeakers.

I'm sure you have had the opportunity to play around with Equalization, at the very least on whatever device you use to listen to music with. You can modify the frequency response of your music by altering the tone controls on your stereo. But it is always good to begin with a starting point that is objective. One song EQ'd one way on a sound device will not necessarily sound as good or the same as on another. That's why we always zero out our board when beginning a new recording. (i.e. set all the levels on all plug-ins and EQ to zero.)

An experienced engineer will save many of their favorite settings for EQ and plug-in effects. Most software plug-ins allow to you to create a certain number of saved pre-sets. Some of these may already be in there, as created by the manufacturer, but there usually is a way for you to save your own. Sort of like the favorites button when you are looking for quick access to your favorite web sites. If your plug-in effects have pre-sets created by the manufacturer, they usually give them creative names that are usually pretty descriptive about what effect they have on the sound.

Try them out-many of my favorites have been discovered that way, and saved me a ton of time in terms of trying to find the sound I'm looking for.

One last point, and this has to do with live sound. No two rooms or venues ever sound the same. Particularly with live sound, the band I was in had to set up anew at any new venue. Each time we had to begin the EQ process over again, and the best place to start was usually with a flat frequency response. Again, experience can provide some insight and shortcuts, but starting from zero was usually a good policy. This can hold true for amplifiers as well. A setting that sounded great in one place, can suddenly sound like absolute crap in another.

In our next chapter we'll break down the frequency spectrum down into distinct parts. That will help us isolate specific frequencies that have their own unique characteristics. It will also make it easier for us to communicate with others about which part of the frequency spectrum we are working with, or trying to fine tune.

Chapter Fourteen: The Frequency Spectrum

In this chapter we'll break the frequency spectrum down into distinct parts. That will help us isolate specific frequencies that have their own unique characteristics. It will also make it easier for us to communicate with others about which part of the frequency spectrum we are working with, or trying to fine tune.

So let's jump right into talking about The Frequency Spectrum. The frequency spectrum, which is sometimes also called bandwidth, can be broken down into three main areas which can be subdivided even further.

For now, let's focus on the three main sections: Bass, midrange, and treble.

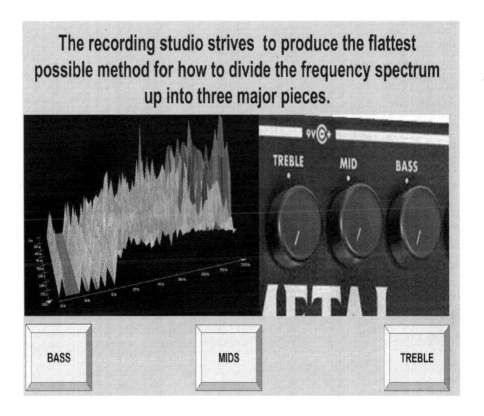

BASS: Approximately 16 to 240 HZ

Deep Bass: 16 to 80 Hz. This area contains the lowest musical notes, room resonance and rumble which can sometimes be felt more than heard. Insufficient levels of deep bass will result in a power-less signal with loss of depth and richness. Such as the electric guitar. It is an area of fatness for many instruments, especially drums. Too little emphasis in this area also reduces the feeling of power.

Upper Bass: 80 to 240 Hz. This area encompasses the high end of bass instruments combined with the low end of midrange instruments.

MIDRANGE: Approximately 240 to 5 kHz.

Low midrange: 240 to 400 Hz. The body of the rhythmic accompaniment in contemporary music lies in this range, especially the richness of the electric guitar.
Central midrange: 500 Hz to 2.5 kHz. This is where the punch and bite occurs in many instruments. Vocals, piano, guitar and drums will tend to sound thin if frequencies in this range are missing or reduced.

Upper midrange: 2.5 kHz to 5 kHz. The topmost notes of the piano and synthesizers are capable of producing notes in the upper midrange, but overtones and harmonics occupy the majority of this area. By increasing levels in this range, presence is accentuated and the brightness of music is preserved.

TREBLE: 5 kHz to 16 kHz

Low treble: there is very little musical information in this range except for some harmonics; the main concern to the engineer is tape hiss.

High treble: 10 kHz to 16 kHz. The fine sizzly high frequency components are present here, in this the final octave of the ten octave frequency system.

In our next chapter, we wrap things up with a discussion of how sound passes through the entire recording chain. This will summarize everything we've learned. We'll look at all the transitions that a sound goes through as it travels from its raw sound to its faithful reproduction. This last chapter will be an overview of the recording and playback of the sound that we have so diligently captured!

Chapter Fifteen: The Recording Chain

In this chapter, we wrap things up with a discussion of how sound passes through the entire recording chain.
Let's take a bit of time to see how sound passes through the recording chain...

In the beginning, vibration causes a sound to be created and generates acoustic waves. Those waves travel through air as acoustical energy much like waves moving across water. These waves are picked up by a microphone , converted into electrical impulses and transmitted through electrical wire, first to amplifiers in the mixing console, then to a recorder which transforms them so that they can stored on a device. The mixing console controls the levels of the inputs from the microphones and steers them onto whichever track (or tracks) of the multi-track recorder is desired.

At a recording session, every musical instrument is designated its own microphone and each of the signals is recorded separately on its own track. By keeping the instruments separated from one another, this allows any balance and tonal changes to be made to any instrument's sound, right up to and including the time of the final mix down. The proportions of volume of each sound can be adjusted by the fader controls in the recording software's console , and each individual tone can be modified by making adjustments at the equalizer section.

Effects plug-ins can also be used to alter the sound of any individual track. There are endless number of plug-ins that do all kinds of amazing things to sound-for now just know that they exist as exploring plug-ins is something that is broader than our scope at this point. You can also decide where to place a given recorded track in the stereo field, by using the panning adjustment to move the signal more towards the right or left channel. However it is usually best not to make this decision until you reach the mix down stage. So keep your channels panned at 12 O'clock when recording!

The microphone may be by-passed if the original signal was electronic and not acoustic. For example, a synthesizer or electric guitar pick-up already produce electrical waves so these instruments do not require a mic and could be plugged directly into a direct injection (DI) box: a device which will match the level of their signal to the ideal acceptance level at the input of the recorder.

From the input console, the signal is sent to the recorder to be stored on disc. Different instruments or sounds need not necessarily be recorded at the same time. But if you only have two inputs into your recorder, you will need some sort of mixer if you are doing live recording which requires more than two inputs.

Later, when the recording is played back, the sounds recorded on disc are still able to be manipulated by the software , which ultimately sends the sounds to the computer interface which translates the sounds and passes them along to external speakers.

Many auxiliary pieces of equipment are introduced by the engineer at various points. In the recording chain to process and modify the sounds in a creative or corrective fashion. For example, echo units, compressors, flangers, etc. There is a big difference between a home studio and a professional studio. Pro studios have expanded capacities to be able to fine tune sound which far exceed home software recording capabilities. While home studios have come to the point where they can produce very professional sounding recordings-they do not have the resources to fine tune sound the way a full blown studio does.

Getting back to the recording chain, signals are sent from the mixing console to the monitor system. In the control room of the recording studio, throughout the recording process, the engineer must be able to accurately hear what has been recorded and what is about to be recorded. This is accomplished by the monitoring system; the loudspeakers, headphones and their associated power amplifiers. The monitor speakers recreate the original sounds once again as acoustical sound waves in the surrounding air via the vibration of their speaker cones.

Let's start things off with a little diagram I made. Here's how it works: Start at the guitar, and follow the arrows through each step in the signal chain, until you arrive at the ear in the center.

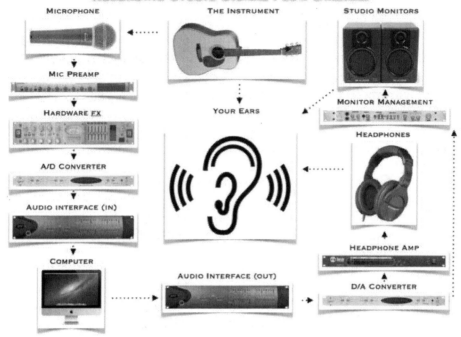

In the MOST complex studio setups, this is the exact path an audio signal must travel to reach your ears.

In simpler studios, you might imagine that the signal flow would be simpler as well. The truth is...it's NOT. It's the same.

Here's why:

Take for example a simple audio interface:

Along with a laptop, a mic, and some monitors, this one box can comprise an entire studio. But within this box, are extremely basic versions of all the other devices outlined in the diagram. The reason you don't need a separate mic preamp or digital converter is that BOTH are contained within the interface. It doesn't mean there are fewer steps in the signal flow. It only means that more steps happen within the same box.

A step by step walk through the diagram:

1.Microphone->Mic Preamp

The microphone picks up the sound, and a mic level signal is sent to the microphone preamp. Since mic level signals are inherently weak, the preamp is needed to amplify it to a higher level. The amplified signal is known as line level.

2. Mic Preamp->Hardware Effects

The mic preamp sends the line level signal to any number of analog signal processors including EQ and compression. This step in the process is optional, and in less expensive studios, is often skipped in favor of digital signal processing within the DAW. (Digital Audio Workstation.)

3.Hardware Effects->A/D Converter

The hardware effects unit sends the processed analog signal to the A/D converter to be translated into a digital audio signal.

4. A/D Converter->Audio Interface->Computer

The A/D converter sends the digital signal to the audio interface, where it is sent into the computer to be processed by the Digital Audio Workstation (DAW). Within the DAW, the signal is processed by any number of inserted plugins, and mixed with any other tracks in the session.

5. Computer->Audio Interface->D/A Converter

After all DAW process is complete, the signal is sent out to the audio interface and passed to the D/A converter, where it is reverted back into an analog signal.

6. D/A Converter->Headphone Amp, Monitor Management

The D/A converter sends the new analog signal to one of two places: either the headphone amp, or monitor management system. This is the final step in the process before converting the signal back into sound.

7. Headphone Amp->Headphones

When the analog signal reaches the headphone amp, it is then sent to the headphones, where it is heard by the performer.

8. Monitor Management System->Studio Monitors

When the analog signal reaches the monitor management system, it is then sent to the studio monitors, where it is heard by the sound engineer.

That, is a simple yet complete summary of the entire recording studio signal flow, start to finish.

Over the course of time, I have found that most of the folks who are interested in this material are musicians, as I am myself. From that standpoint, perhaps you will understand that the information here is analogous to studying the theory of music. You don't need to know the theory in order to play music, but once you understand the theory, you have much more control over your ability to play and express your thoughts in a much more accurate fashion.

 Now that we have summarized the signal flow of the recording process, we have reached a decisive point in our learning. You now have the foundational background to understand how sound works. This knowledge gives you a leg up when it comes to recording, because you understand the properties of the medium you are working with. Congratulations on completing this fundamental study of the basics of sound for recording. Bear in mind that the better you know the behavior of what it is you are trying to capture, the more successful you will be at capturing it in its finest form! So long, and thanks so much for joining me on this adventure to capture the best sound possible!

Made in the USA
San Bernardino, CA
26 May 2018